How to Hire the Right One

Henry Allen

Copyright Page

Publisher: Univon

Release Year 2025

Index

The Impact of a Bad Hire

Hiring the wrong person isn't just a small administrative error; it's a problem that can affect the entire company, from the work environment to the bottom line. At first glance, a bad employee may seem like a minor annoyance, but over time, the negative effects accumulate and can wreak havoc on the team, customers, and business results. It's like a small hole in a ship that, if left untreated, can sink.

When a company hires someone who doesn't fit the position or the organizational culture, the first impact is felt on productivity. A poor employee may take longer than expected to complete tasks, make frequent mistakes, or even not do their job well. This forces other team members to cover for their shortcomings, leading to frustration and discontent. Instead of moving forward efficiently, the team wastes time fixing the problems caused by that person.

The impact on the work environment is another major issue. A bad employee can bring with them negative attitudes, lack of commitment, or even conflicts with other colleagues. If a team member is toxic, unmotivated, or irresponsible, it can affect everyone's morale. Teamwork weakens, tensions rise, and in the worst-case scenario, the best employees end up quitting because they don't want to deal with a difficult environment. A single negative element can be enough for a solid team to begin to deteriorate.

From a financial perspective, a bad hire is a waste of money. You invest in training, salary, and benefits, only to find that the person isn't adding value. If you have to fire and replace someone, the selection process, interviews, and training of a new candidate generate additional costs. In some industries, the financial damage can be even greater if the bad hire makes costly mistakes, damages the company's reputation, or even causes the loss of important clients.

The impact on customers is also a risk that shouldn't be ignored. If an employee with a bad attitude serves customers, they're likely to have a bad experience and not return. Poor service can lead to negative comments, negative reviews, and a damaged company image. In the age of social media, a single bad experience shared by a dissatisfied customer can cause significant damage to a business's reputation.

Furthermore, a bad hire forces a company to lose focus on what's truly important. Instead of concentrating on growth, innovation, and improvement, time is wasted trying to solve problems caused by a poor choice. Leaders' and managers' energy is diverted into managing conflicts, correcting mistakes, and, ultimately, finding a solution to replace the employee who never should have been hired.

The worst part is that a bad hire often isn't detected immediately. It's a problem that worsens over time. At first, it may seem like the person just needs a little adaptation or more training, but over the months, it becomes clear that they're not a good fit. By the time the company realizes it needs to make a change, it has already lost valuable resources, time, and, in some cases, even other key employees who left out of frustration at working with someone who wasn't supposed to be there.

That's why hiring the right candidate from the start is one of the most important decisions in any business. It's not just about filling a position as quickly as possible, but about finding someone who truly adds value, fits into the company culture, and helps build a strong team. Because when a company hires poorly, it pays the price in many ways—and in some cases, that price is too high.

Defining the Ideal Profile

Hiring the right employee begins long before posting a job posting or conducting an interview. It all starts with defining exactly what type of person is needed for the position. This step is critical because, if the ideal candidate profile isn't clear, the selection process becomes a guessing game in which you run the risk of hiring someone who isn't a good fit.

Defining the ideal profile doesn't just mean listing technical requirements, such as degrees or experience. A common mistake is focusing solely on hard skills and forgetting that attitude, personality, and adaptability are equally important. An employee with the best resume in the world may not be the best choice if they don't share the company's values or if their way of working doesn't fit with the team's.

The first step in defining the ideal profile is understanding exactly what the business needs. It's not just about filling a vacancy, but about finding someone who truly adds value. To do this, you need to analyze in detail what tasks the person will perform, what skills are essential, and what type of personality best fits the team. Hiring a salesperson, who needs to be outgoing and persuasive, is not the same as hiring an accountant, who needs to be organized and meticulous.

Another key aspect is determining the minimum experience and knowledge the candidate should have. Companies often make two opposing mistakes: asking for too many requirements or not asking for enough. If the list of requirements is excessive, they risk losing good candidates who could learn on the job. But if someone is hired without adequate training, the learning curve can be excessively long and costly. The key is to find a balance between what is needed and what is possible to achieve in the labor market.

Company culture also plays a fundamental role in defining the ideal profile. Every organization has its own work style, values, and way of doing things. If a candidate doesn't fit into that environment, no matter how talented they are, they're likely to feel uncomfortable and may end up resigning or causing conflict. Therefore, it's important to define what type of person best suits the company's way of working. If it's a dynamic environment with constant change, someone flexible and proactive is needed. If it's a more structured environment where strict processes are followed, the ideal candidate is someone who prefers stability and order.

An often overlooked element is the candidate's potential within the company. It's not just about hiring someone who can do the job today, but someone who can grow and contribute in the future. It's advisable to consider how that person might develop within the organization, what skills they can acquire over time, and whether they have the attitude to learn and improve. A candidate with potential can be more valuable than someone with experience but no desire to evolve.

To define the ideal profile, it's helpful to make a list of three categories: essential requirements, desirable skills, and personal characteristics. Essential requirements are those without which the candidate couldn't do the job, such as technical knowledge or specific experience. Desirable skills are those that aren't essential but can make a difference, such as additional software skills or experience in a related sector. Personal characteristics include aspects such as attitude, teamwork skills, and stress tolerance.

Taking the time to accurately define the ideal profile before beginning the candidate search makes the entire hiring process more efficient. It reduces the number of unnecessary interviews, attracts the right candidates, and prevents the mistake of hiring someone just because they seemed like a good fit at the time. A company that knows exactly who it's looking for is much more likely to find the right person and build a strong, successful team.

Creating an Attractive Job Offer

Posting a job offer isn't simply a matter of writing an ad with a list of requirements and responsibilities. If you want to attract the best candidates, the offer must be clear, compelling, and convey the true value of working for the company. A poorly written or overly generic offer can cause ideal candidates to ignore it or cause them to only apply for people who don't really fit the needs.

The first step in creating an effective job offer is to have a clear profile of the ideal candidate. You can't attract the right person if you don't know exactly what you're looking for. It's important to clearly define the necessary skills, the required experience, and, above all, the personal characteristics that would make the candidate a good fit for the company. With this in mind, the job offer should be written in a way that sparks interest in those who fit the profile and automatically filters out those who don't fit the requirements.

The title of the job posting is one of the most important elements. A generic or unclear title can cause the ad to go unnoticed among hundreds of similar postings. It's a good idea to use a title that accurately and compellingly describes the position. Instead of writing something vague like "Assistant Wanted," it's better to specify "Administrative Assistant with Customer Service Experience." This helps suitable candidates quickly identify if the position is right for them.

After the title, the introduction to the job offer should immediately grab the candidate's attention. Instead of starting with a long list of requirements, it's better to begin with a brief description of the company and the impact the position will have within the organization. People aren't just looking for a job; they also want to feel part of something important. Explaining in a few lines why the company is a good place to work and how the position contributes to business growth makes the offer much more attractive.

In the responsibilities section, it's essential to be specific without being overwhelming. A common mistake is writing an endless list of duties, which can make the offer seem unattractive or confusing. Instead, it's best to highlight the five or six most important responsibilities of the position. This allows the candidate to have a clear idea of what will be expected of them without feeling intimidated by an overly long list.

Job requirements should also be presented strategically. If you include too many requirements, you risk scaring away qualified candidates who may not meet all the requirements but could learn quickly. The best practice is to separate requirements into two categories: must-haves and nice-to-haves. Must-haves are those that are truly needed for the position, such as experience in a specific area or mastery of certain tools. Nice-to-haves are additional skills that would be an asset but are not essential to the job.

One of the factors that most influences candidates' decisions is the salary offer and benefits. Many companies make the mistake of not including salary information, which can cause the best candidates to pass them by. While it's not always necessary to specify an exact number, at least a salary range should be offered so that candidates have a clear idea of what they can expect. In addition to salary, it's important to mention benefits such as bonuses, growth opportunities, training, or any other incentives that make the job more attractive.

The tone of the job offer is also key. An offer that is too formal and cold can make the company seem rigid or unwelcoming. On the other hand, an overly casual tone can give the impression that the job is not serious. The ideal is to find a balance, using professional yet friendly language that conveys confidence and reflects the company culture.

Finally, it's essential to include clear instructions on how to apply. Indicate whether candidates must submit a resume, fill out a form, or include a cover letter. It's also helpful to establish a deadline for receiving applications and mention the selection process, such as whether there will be online interviews or additional tests.

A well-crafted job posting not only attracts the best candidates, but also helps reduce the number of irrelevant applications, making the selection process more efficient. Taking the time to write it clearly and strategically is an investment that can make the difference between finding the perfect employee or wasting time with candidates who don't really fit the needs.

Where to Find the Best Candidates

Finding the best candidates isn't a matter of luck or waiting for the right person to magically appear. Attracting quality talent requires knowing exactly where to look and how to do so strategically. If you post a job opening anywhere without a plan, you risk receiving hundreds of irrelevant applications or, worse yet, not finding anyone truly qualified for the position.

The first place to look for candidates is within the company itself. Often, the best option to fill a vacancy already works within the organization. Promoting someone from the team or giving an employee the opportunity to take on new responsibilities not only saves time and money in the selection process, but also motivates employees by showing them that there are opportunities for growth. Before going out to the market to find someone new, it's always a good idea to analyze whether there's someone internal who could fill the position.

If there isn't a suitable candidate within the company, the next option is to use online employment platforms. Specialized job posting websites are one of the most effective ways to reach a large pool of candidates in a short amount of time. Platforms like LinkedIn, Indeed, or Glassdoor allow you to filter applicants based on experience, location, and skills, making it easier to find people who truly fit the desired profile. However, it's not enough to simply post a job and wait. It's advisable to actively review profiles, directly contact people who seem suitable, and participate in groups or forums where industry professionals interact.

Social media can also be a powerful tool for finding talent. Posting the job opening on your company's LinkedIn, Facebook, or even Twitter pages can help reach more people, especially if current employees share it with their networks. Often, the best candidates aren't actively looking for work, but if they see an interesting opportunity on their social networks, they may be drawn to apply or recommend someone who fits the profile.

Another effective strategy is the use of employee referrals. Many companies have found that candidates recommended by current employees tend to be more trustworthy and fit better into the organizational culture. Asking employees to recommend people from their professional networks can generate high-quality applications. Some companies even offer incentives to employees who refer candidates who are eventually hired and remain with the company for a specified period.

Job fairs and networking events are also excellent opportunities to find talent. In these spaces, you can meet candidates face-to-face, assess their attitude and skills in real time, and make more personal connections that go beyond a simple resume. Participating in industry events, conferences, or speaking engagements can also help identify professionals who excel in their field and could be a great addition to your team.

Another option not to be overlooked is contacting universities and training institutes. If you're looking for young talent with growth potential, working with educational institutions can be a great strategy. Many universities have job boards or internship programs where companies can find students or recent graduates eager to learn and contribute new ideas. Although these candidates may not have much experience, their enthusiasm and willingness to learn can make them an excellent long-term investment.

For more specialized or high-level positions, recruiting agencies can be an effective solution. These agencies have databases of pre-screened candidates and can help find people with the exact skills needed. Although their service comes at a cost, it can be a time-saving investment that ensures only truly qualified candidates are interviewed.

Finally, a strategy that is increasingly being used is proactive recruiting. Instead of waiting for candidates to apply, companies can identify talented individuals on LinkedIn or other platforms and contact them directly. Sometimes the best employees are already working elsewhere, but if they receive an attractive offer, they may be willing to change companies.

Finding the best candidates isn't a passive process; it requires planning and a combination of different strategies. Companies that know where and how to look are more likely to attract quality talent, reduce hiring time, and build strong teams that contribute to business growth. In a competitive job market, successful hiring depends not only on posting a job opening, but also on knowing how and where to find the right person.

Filtering Resumes and First Contact

Receiving a large number of resumes isn't necessarily a good sign if you don't have a clear system for filtering them. Reviewing each application in a disorganized manner can waste time and lead to hiring the wrong person. Therefore, it's essential to establish an efficient process for filtering resumes and selecting only candidates with true potential before moving on to the next stage.

The first step is to be clear about the essential requirements of the position. Before reading a single resume, you should review the previously defined ideal profile description. This way, it's easier to identify which candidates meet the basic requirements and which can be discarded immediately. It's important to remember that the idea isn't to find the best candidate as quickly as possible, but to ensure that only those who are truly a good fit for the position make it to the next stage.

An effective strategy for screening resumes is to use a categorization system. These can be divided into three main groups: candidates who meet all the essential requirements, candidates who meet some but could make up for it with other skills, and candidates who fall short. Resumes in the latter group should be discarded without delay, while those in the latter group can be analyzed in more detail to assess whether their potential warrants moving forward in the process.

One of the most common mistakes when reviewing resumes is focusing solely on work experience and academic qualifications. While these elements are important, they don't always reflect a candidate's true skills. It's advisable to pay attention to other details, such as job stability, progression of responsibilities in previous jobs, and any evidence of initiative or continuous learning. A candidate who has grown in their career and demonstrated commitment in previous jobs may be a better choice than someone with a long list of jobs held in short periods.

Another key point is to evaluate the presentation and clarity of the resume. A poorly structured document, with spelling errors, or lacking clear information can be a sign of carelessness or a lack of professionalism. A good resume should be clear, direct, and easy to read. It's not about judging someone solely by format, but if a candidate hasn't taken the time to present their information well, they may have the same attitude toward their job.

Once the resumes have been filtered and the most promising candidates have been selected, it's time to make the first contact. This stage is crucial because it's the candidate's first direct impression of the company. A poorly structured message or call can cause even the best candidate to lose interest in the offer.

The first contact should be brief, clear, and professional. If it's a phone call, you should begin by introducing yourself, mentioning the company's name, and explaining that the candidate's resume has been selected to advance in the hiring process. It's advisable to confirm that the person is still interested in the position before continuing with further details. If the answer is affirmative, you can explain the next step in the process, such as an initial interview or a technical test.

If the initial contact is by email, the message should be equally concise and friendly. It should include the candidate's name, the position being considered for, and a clear invitation to the next step. It's advisable to add details about the selection process so the candidate knows what to expect. It's also helpful to provide a schedule option so the person can confirm availability without unnecessary email exchanges.

Something many companies overlook is the importance of tone during initial contact. If the message is too cold or impersonal, it can generate disinterest. If it's too informal, it can seem unserious. The ideal is to convey professionalism and enthusiasm, making it clear that the company values candidates and that the selection process is well-structured.

The first contact is also an opportunity to assess certain aspects of the candidate before the interview. If the person displays disinterest, a lack of clarity in their speech, or a negative attitude during the call, this could be a red flag. If they respond to the email in a careless manner or with obvious errors, this could also indicate that they are not the type of employee you are looking for.

Screening resumes and making initial contact with candidates is a fundamental step in the hiring process. If done well, it saves time, avoids interviewing people who don't meet the requirements, and creates a better experience for both the company and the applicants. Taking the time to do this strategically increases the chances of finding the right person for the job and reduces the risk of a bad hire.

Effective Interviews

The interview is the key moment in the hiring process. It's the opportunity to really get to know the candidates, assess whether they have the necessary skills, and, most importantly, determine if they fit the company culture. However, many interviews are conducted haphazardly, without a clear strategy, which can lead to poor decisions. For an interview to be effective, it must be well-structured, focus on what really matters, and allow for a fair and objective evaluation of candidates.

Before conducting any interview, it's essential to prepare. It's not just about asking random questions, but about being clear about what you want to discover about the candidate. You should review the job profile again and define the criteria that will be used to evaluate each person. This includes not only technical skills but also aspects such as attitude, problem-solving ability, and compatibility with the team.

The interview environment is also important. If the candidate feels uncomfortable or under too much pressure, they are likely not to show their true potential. An effective interview should allow the person to express themselves naturally, without feeling like they are being interrogated. To achieve this, it is advisable to begin with a friendly introduction, explain the purpose of the interview, and provide an overview of the selection process. This helps build trust and makes the conversation flow better.

The questions asked in the interview determine the quality of the information obtained. Interviewers often resort to generic questions like "What are your strengths and weaknesses?" or "Tell me about yourself," which don't provide any truly useful information. Instead, it's better to ask specific questions based on real-life situations. For example, instead of asking if a candidate can work under pressure, you can ask them to describe an experience in which they had to handle a stressful situation and how they resolved it.

A very effective approach is behavioral questions, which are based on the idea that the best predictor of future behavior is past behavior. These types of questions force the candidate to provide concrete examples of how they have handled situations in the past. Questions like "Tell me about a time you had a conflict with a coworker and how you resolved it" or "Describe a time you had to make a difficult decision at work" can reveal much more about the person than rehearsed answers about their supposed strengths.

It's also important to assess the technical skills needed for the position. Depending on the type of job, this may include hands-on testing, case resolution, or specific technical questions. For example, if you're interviewing a programmer, it's a good idea to ask them to solve a small live coding problem. If you're looking for a salesperson, you might ask them to simulate a customer call. These types of tests help you see how the candidate actually performs in situations similar to those they'll face on the job.

A candidate's attitude is a key factor that shouldn't be overlooked. Beyond their knowledge and experience, it's important to observe how they respond to questions, their body language, and their level of interest in the position. A candidate who responds enthusiastically, asks questions about the company, and shows initiative will likely have a better attitude at work than someone who answers in a monotonous manner or shows little interest.

Another important point is compatibility with the company culture. It's not enough for a candidate to be technically competent if their way of working clashes with the organization's values and style. To assess this, you can ask questions about how they like to work, what kind of environment they prefer, or how they handle change and pressure. You can also use the interview to discuss the company culture and observe the candidate's reaction. If their attitude and values don't match those of the organization, they likely won't fit well with the team.

During the interview, it's a good idea to take detailed notes so you can compare candidates objectively later. It's easy to forget important details when you've conducted multiple interviews in one day, so recording observations about attitude, responses, and any relevant points helps you make a better decision at the end of the interview.

Finally, the closing of the interview is just as important as the beginning. It's advisable to give the candidate the opportunity to ask questions, as this allows you to gauge their level of interest and clarify any concerns they may have. It's also important to explain the next steps in the selection process and give them an idea of how long it will take to receive a response. A well-informed candidate will feel more valued and have a better impression of the company, which increases the likelihood of accepting an offer if selected.

A well-conducted interview not only serves to evaluate candidates, but is also an opportunity to project a positive image of the company and generate interest in the position. By following a structured process, asking relevant questions, and focusing on what really matters, you can make better decisions and increase the likelihood of hiring the right person.

Beyond the CV

Hiring someone based solely on their resume is a mistake many companies make. While a resume is a useful tool for learning about a candidate's education and work experience, it doesn't tell everything about the person. A job title can't reflect aspects such as attitude, adaptability, work ethic, or how someone handles problems. Therefore, to make a good hiring decision, it's necessary to go beyond the resume and evaluate the candidate from different angles.

One of the most important aspects missing from a resume is the candidate's attitude. Many companies have hired people with a wealth of degrees and experience, only to discover they have a poor attitude, are poor team players, or lack interest in learning. Attitude is key because skills can be taught, but willingness and commitment depend on the individual. A candidate who demonstrates enthusiasm, asks intelligent questions, and shows genuine interest in the company is often a better choice than someone with an impressive resume who appears indifferent or unmotivated.

Adaptability is another crucial factor that can't be assessed with a resume alone. In an ever-changing world of work, companies need employees who can learn quickly, adapt to new circumstances, and handle unforeseen situations. A candidate with years of experience in a single type of job, but without the flexibility to face new challenges, may be left behind when the business evolves. To assess adaptability, it's advisable to ask questions about how the candidate has handled changes in previous jobs, what they've learned in difficult situations, and how they cope with challenges.

Another aspect that is often overlooked is compatibility with the company culture. Every company has a unique work style and values that define its work environment. Some companies encourage autonomy and creativity, while others value structure and strict adherence to procedures. A candidate may be excellent in terms of skills, but if their personality and values don't fit the company culture, they are likely to feel uncomfortable in their job and their performance may not be as expected. To avoid this, it's helpful to discuss the company culture during the interview and observe the candidate's reaction.

Emotional intelligence is another key factor that can't be measured on a resume. A candidate with an impeccable professional record may struggle with stress management, conflict resolution, or effective communication with colleagues. Emotional intelligence is the ability to understand and manage one's own emotions and those of others, and is essential for working well in a team. To assess this aspect, you can ask questions about how the candidate has handled conflicts in the past, how they react to criticism, and how they feel working under pressure.

Work ethic is also difficult to measure with a resume alone, but it can make the difference between a reliable employee and one who causes problems. A candidate with a long list of accomplishments on their resume isn't always someone committed and responsible. Some people have changed jobs many times because they don't fulfill their responsibilities or because they have a negative attitude toward their work. To detect this, it's important to analyze the candidate's work history and ask questions about how they manage their time, how they prioritize their tasks, and how they ensure they meet their commitments.

Continuous learning is another aspect that isn't always reflected on a resume, but is essential in today's world. A candidate who settles for what they already know and doesn't seek to improve can quickly fall behind. On the other hand, someone who constantly seeks to learn new skills and improve their performance will be a valuable asset to the company. To assess this aspect, you can ask questions about what books, courses, or experiences have helped the candidate grow professionally and what new skills they would like to learn in the future.

A resume can tell a lot about a candidate, but it never tells the whole story. To make a good hiring decision, it's necessary to look beyond the paper and evaluate the whole person. Attitude, adaptability, emotional intelligence, work ethic, and desire to learn are factors that can make the difference between an average employee and one who truly adds value to the company. A selection process that takes these aspects into account will not only reduce the risk of a bad hire, but will also help build a stronger, more engaged team.

Detecting Lies and Exaggerations

Hiring the wrong person can be costly for a company, and one of the main reasons this happens is because some candidates lie or exaggerate on their resumes and in interviews. While most people present their experience and skills in the best possible light, some go further and falsify information to appear more qualified than they really are. Detecting these lies and exaggerations is critical to avoiding hiring someone who lacks the necessary skills or who is dishonest from the outset.

One of the most common places where candidates lie is in their work experience. Some people inflate the positions they've held, exaggerate their responsibilities, or even invent jobs they've never had. To detect this type of deception, it's important to carefully review the details of the resume and be alert for inconsistencies. If a candidate has changed jobs many times in short periods or if there are unexplained gaps in their work history, this is a red flag. An effective way to verify experience is to ask for references and contact previous employers directly. Companies can confirm whether they actually worked there and what type of responsibilities they had.

Another area where candidates often lie is their skills. It's common for some people to claim to be proficient in programs, languages, or techniques they actually barely understand. An easy way to detect this is to ask specific questions in the interview. If someone claims to be proficient in a language, you can ask them a question in that language to see how they respond. If they claim to have advanced knowledge of a software, you can ask them to explain how to solve a problem with that tool. It's also helpful to include a short technical test in the selection process to verify that they really have the skills they claim to have.

Employment dates are another area where candidates often adjust their work history to make their track record appear more solid. Some stretch the dates of their previous jobs to hide periods of unemployment or to make it appear they were in a position longer than they actually were. If a candidate says they worked at a company for five years, but when contacted, the company confirms they only worked for two, it's a clear sign they've altered their record.

Academic degrees and certifications can also be falsified or exaggerated. Some people claim to have earned degrees they didn't actually complete or mention courses they never took. To avoid this problem, it's advisable to ask for official documentation to back up the information. Many educational institutions allow you to verify whether someone actually graduated from them, so it's a good idea to do so in cases where the degree is key to the position.

Fake references are another common problem. Some candidates use friends or family members as references who are willing to lie for them, posing as former bosses or coworkers. To avoid this, it's important to contact the company where they supposedly worked directly and ask to speak to someone in the human resources department or a real supervisor. It's also helpful to ask the reference detailed questions, such as exact dates of employment and specific responsibilities, to see if the information is consistent with what the candidate said in the interview.

The candidate's demeanor during the interview can also provide clues as to whether they are lying or exaggerating. When someone lies, they tend to avoid specific details and give very general answers. For example, if you ask them about a project they worked on and they only respond in vague terms without providing specific examples, they may not be telling the truth. It's also common for people who exaggerate to talk excessively about their accomplishments and minimize any difficulties they've faced in the past.

Another strategy for detecting lies is to ask repeated questions at different times during the interview or during various stages of the selection process. If a candidate lies, they'll likely have difficulty remembering exactly what they said before and end up giving contradictory answers. A good interviewer can notice these inconsistencies and ask additional questions to confirm the information.

Social media and profiles on platforms like LinkedIn can be a valuable tool for verifying a candidate's information. If a candidate claims to have worked at a company for several years but their LinkedIn profile contains different information, or if they have no connections to former colleagues from that job, it could be a sign that something isn't right.

While detecting lies and exaggerations in a hiring process can take time and effort, it's a necessary investment to avoid problems in the future. A candidate who lies on their resume or in an interview likely won't be a trustworthy employee. Asking strategic questions, checking references, and being alert for signs of inconsistencies can make the difference between hiring the right person or making a costly mistake.

The Importance of Corporate Culture

Every company has its own way of doing things. Beyond the products or services it offers, there is a set of values, beliefs, and behaviors that determine how work is done within the organization. This is what is known as company culture, and although it is sometimes overlooked in hiring processes, its importance cannot be underestimated. Hiring someone who doesn't fit the company culture can cause long-term problems, even if the candidate has all the necessary skills for the position.

Company culture influences how employees interact with each other, how decisions are made, and the overall work environment. Some companies value autonomy and creativity, allowing employees to propose new ideas and work independently. Other companies prefer more rigid structures, where each person follows specific procedures without deviating from them. No approach is better than another, but it's critical that new employees adapt well to the way the company operates.

A common problem in many companies is hiring based solely on experience and technical skills, without considering whether the person will be comfortable with the organizational culture. A candidate may be excellent at their job, but if their values, attitude, or work style clash with the company culture, they're likely to end up leaving or causing conflict within the team. For example, if a company has a relaxed and collaborative work environment but hires someone who prefers to work alone and follow strict orders, they're likely to be a poor fit and underperform.

Company culture also has a direct impact on employee motivation and productivity. When a person identifies with the company's values and way of working, they feel more engaged and motivated. Conversely, if there is a disconnect between what the company stands for and what employees seek in their work environment, their engagement level will be low and their performance will suffer. An employee who feels out of place will not only be less productive but can also negatively impact the morale of the entire team.

Another important point is that company culture plays a key role in talent retention. If a company wants to avoid high employee turnover, it needs to ensure that the people it hires fit with its philosophy and work style. Often, people don't leave their jobs because they don't like what they do, but because they don't feel comfortable with the way the company operates or the way relationships are handled within the team. When there is good alignment between employees and company culture, job satisfaction is higher and people are less likely to look for opportunities elsewhere.

To ensure a candidate is a good fit for the company culture, it's important to ask specific questions during the selection process. Questions like "How do you like to work in a team?", "What kind of work environment motivates you most?", or "What values do you consider important in a company?" can give a clear idea of whether the person shares the same vision as the organization. It's also helpful to describe the company culture during the interview and observe the candidate's reaction. If they appear enthusiastic and ask questions about the way of working, that's a good sign. If they seem indifferent or uncomfortable, it may be a sign they're not the right person for the position.

Another important aspect is that company culture should not only be defined in words, but should be reflected in the company's day-to-day operations. If a company says it values innovation but discourages any new ideas from employees, its actual culture is very different from what it claims. It is essential that the organization's leaders lead by example and that internal policies support the values the company promotes. Company culture must be consistent and authentic to truly have a positive impact on hiring and employee performance.

Furthermore, company culture can be a differentiating factor in attracting talent. Many people look for more than just a salary and financial benefits when choosing a job. They want to work in a place where they feel valued, where they can grow, and where the work environment is pleasant. Companies with a well-defined and attractive culture can attract candidates who identify with their way of doing things, which increases the likelihood of finding committed and loyal employees.

Building and maintaining a strong company culture is neither an automatic nor a simple process. It requires constant effort to ensure that everyone in the organization understands and practices it on a daily basis. But when achieved, the benefits are enormous. A company with a strong culture will not only attract and retain better talent, but will also have happier, more motivated, and more productive employees. The key is to understand that culture is not a minor detail in the hiring process, but a determining factor in the company's long-term success.

Growth Potential Assessment

When a company hires someone, it's not just looking for someone who can do the job now, but also someone who can grow and add more value over time. Evaluating a candidate's growth potential is key to building a strong team and ensuring the organization's long-term success. It's not just about finding someone with the right experience and skills, but also about identifying who has the capacity and motivation to learn, adapt, and take on greater responsibilities in the future.

A candidate's growth potential isn't always evident on their resume. There may be individuals with an impressive work history who have actually reached their professional ceiling and show no interest in further learning. On the other hand, there are candidates who may have less experience but have a great learning capacity and a strong desire to improve. To assess this potential, it's necessary to go beyond degrees and certifications and analyze aspects such as attitude, intellectual curiosity, and problem-solving skills.

One of the clearest indicators of a candidate's growth potential is their desire to learn. People with a growth mindset constantly seek to improve their skills, whether by taking courses, reading about their industry, or looking for ways to improve their performance. During the interview, questions such as "What was the last new skill you learned and how did you do it?", "How do you stay current in your field?", or "How do you react when faced with a problem you don't know how to solve?" can reveal whether the candidate has a learning-oriented mindset or prefers to stay in their comfort zone.

Adaptability is another key factor in growth potential. In a world where technology and industries change rapidly, companies need employees who can adapt to new circumstances without difficulty. A candidate who has changed sectors or taken on various roles throughout their career can demonstrate the flexibility to learn new things and adapt to unexpected changes. To assess this, you can ask questions about situations in which the candidate had to break from their routine, learn something new quickly, or change their approach to adapt to a different environment.

Another important aspect is the ability to solve problems independently. A candidate with high potential not only follows instructions but is also able to analyze situations, identify solutions, and make decisions effectively. To measure this ability, you can present hypothetical scenarios during the interview and ask the candidate to explain how they would solve them. If the response is structured, logical, and demonstrates initiative, it is a good sign that the candidate has the potential to take on greater responsibilities in the future.

Leadership is another indicator of growth potential. Not everyone aspires to be a manager or director, but the ability to influence others, work as part of a team, and take initiative are valuable traits in any organization. A candidate with leadership skills shows interest in helping colleagues, proposing ideas, and taking on responsibilities without being asked. During the selection process, questions such as "Have you ever taken the lead on a project without being asked?" or "How do you handle situations where someone on your team is struggling?" can be asked. If the candidate demonstrates they have been able to lead in the past, they will likely be able to do so on a larger scale in the future.

Perseverance and resilience are also factors that indicate a candidate's growth potential. People who can handle failure, learn from mistakes, and move forward with determination are more likely to advance in their careers. To assess this, you can ask questions like, "Tell me about a time you faced a major challenge at work and how you overcame it," or "What was the biggest obstacle you've faced in your career, and what did you learn from it?" A high-potential candidate will view problems as learning opportunities rather than reasons to give up.

Compatibility with the company's vision and values also influences a candidate's growth potential. A person who identifies with the company's mission and is motivated by what it stands for will be more willing to contribute to the organization's growth. To identify this, you can ask questions about what the candidate looks for in a job, what motivates them to give their best, and how they envision their professional development in the coming years. If their answers align with the direction the company wants to move in, it's a sign they could become a valuable long-term asset.

The process of assessing growth potential isn't about finding the perfect candidate, but rather finding someone who has the disposition, attitude, and skills necessary to evolve within the company. Hiring someone with experience may be helpful in the short term, but hiring someone with great potential ensures that the company will have talent capable of taking on new challenges in the future. Identifying these individuals from the selection stage is key to building teams that not only do their jobs well but also help the company grow with them.

How to Compare and Choose the Best Candidate

Selecting the best candidate is no easy task, especially when there are several profiles that meet the job requirements. Often, after reviewing resumes, conducting interviews, and checking references, two or three finalists remain who seem equally qualified. At this point, making the right decision is crucial, as it affects not only the new employee's efficiency but also the stability and growth of the company. To make an effective comparison and choose with confidence, it is necessary to follow a structured process that allows each option to be evaluated fairly and objectively.

The first step in comparing candidates is to thoroughly review their skills and experience. While all finalists may meet the basic requirements of the position, there are always differences in the depth and quality of their experience. It's helpful to make a comparison table with the most important aspects, such as technical knowledge, specific skills, achievements in previous jobs, and length of experience in similar roles. This helps to better visualize which candidate has a clear advantage in terms of qualifications. However, it's important to remember that experience alone isn't always the deciding factor.

Beyond experience, it's essential to assess each candidate's soft skills. Aspects such as communication, problem-solving skills, teamwork, and adaptability are just as important as technical knowledge, especially in companies where collaboration and innovation play a key role. To compare these skills, you can review the interview responses and analyze who demonstrated the best responsiveness, who had a more logical approach, and who conveyed the greatest confidence in their abilities.

Another important factor is compatibility with the company culture. Even if a candidate has the best technical skills, if they don't fit with the organization's way of working, conflicts are likely to arise or their performance may not be as expected. To assess this, you can analyze how each finalist responded to questions about values, work environment, and job expectations. It's also helpful to consider the attitude they displayed throughout the selection process. An enthusiastic and motivated candidate is generally a better choice than someone with an excellent resume but no obvious interest in the company.

Growth potential should also be a key criterion in the comparison. It's not just about choosing the person best suited to the job today, but someone who has the ability and willingness to take on greater responsibilities in the future. To assess this, you can review aspects such as their desire to learn, their track record of professional development, and their interest in continuing to grow within the company. A candidate who shows ambition to continually improve and learn may be a better long-term investment than someone who, although competent, has no interest in professional advancement.

Job references are another key tool in the comparison process. Calling former bosses or supervisors and asking about each candidate's performance, attitude, and reliability can help confirm strengths and identify potential problems. It's important to pay attention to the details in references' responses. If a former boss gives a glowing recommendation and mentions specific accomplishments, it's a positive sign. If, on the other hand, the recommendation is vague or unconvincing, it may be a warning that the candidate wasn't as strong a performer as they claim.

In some cases, it can be helpful to involve others in the final decision. If the position involves teamwork, seeking input from those who will be the candidate's direct reports can provide additional perspective. It's also advisable to involve company leaders in the evaluation, especially if it's a key position within the organization. Having diverse perspectives can prevent bias and help make a more balanced decision.

If, after the entire process, there are still doubts between two or more candidates, an effective strategy is to conduct a practical test or a final interview focused on real-life job situations. Asking finalists to solve a problem or present a proposal on a specific topic can reveal significant differences in their approach, creativity, and skills for the position. Sometimes, a short additional test is enough to make one candidate stand out from the rest.

Ultimately, the decision should be made considering not only objective data but also intuition and the overall impression each candidate left. Hiring someone isn't just a logical act based on scores and comparisons, but also a process in which confidence and certainty in the choice play an important role. If a candidate meets all the requirements but there were doubts or red flags during the interview, it's best to reconsider your choice. Conversely, if someone proved to be the best in almost every aspect and also left a positive impression on the team, they're likely the right person for the position.

Selecting the best candidate doesn't mean seeking perfection, but rather finding the person who has the skills, attitude, and compatibility necessary to add long-term value to the company. A structured and well-thought-out comparison process not only increases the likelihood of making the best decision, but also helps reduce risks and ensure the company has a solid and efficient team.

Making an Irresistible Offer

Once you've finally found the ideal candidate, the next step is getting them to agree to join your company. To do this, it's essential to make them an irresistible offer, something that will motivate them to choose your proposal over any other they may have. Many employers and recruiters assume that offering a good salary is enough, but the reality is that professionals are looking for much more than money. They want to feel valued, have opportunities for growth, and work in an environment where they truly enjoy what they do. A well-designed offer should not only be financially attractive but also connect with the candidate's expectations, interests, and aspirations.

The first key aspect of an irresistible offer is clarity. The proposal must be precise and detailed, leaving no room for doubt or ambiguous interpretation. The candidate must know exactly how much they will earn, what benefits they will have, what their schedule will be like, what expectations there are for their performance, and what growth opportunities they will have within the company. When the offer is vague or incomplete, the candidate may feel insecure and begin to consider other options.

Salary is undoubtedly an important factor, but it's not always the deciding factor for a candidate. Often, professionals will accept offers with slightly lower compensation if the benefits package and working conditions are sufficiently attractive. This is where aspects such as performance bonuses, additional days off, remote work options, professional development plans, and any other incentives that make the offer more comprehensive come into play. If the company can't offer a very high salary, it should compensate for it with other elements that make the proposal difficult to refuse.

One of the benefits most valued by candidates is work flexibility. The ability to work from home on certain days, have more flexible hours, or have special leave to attend to personal matters can make the difference between accepting or rejecting an offer. In a world where work-life balance is increasingly important, companies that offer greater flexibility have a competitive advantage in attracting talent.

Opportunities for professional growth and development also play a crucial role in an irresistible offer. A candidate with ambition and a desire to advance not only seeks a good salary, but also the opportunity to learn, improve their skills, and advance their career. Including training programs, access to specialized courses, opportunities for internal promotion, and mentorship with company professionals in the offer can make the candidate view the job as an investment in their future.

Another factor that makes an offer more attractive is the company's culture. If the candidate has shown interest in the organization's way of working and its values, it's important to reinforce this aspect when presenting the offer. You can talk about the work environment, team dynamics, innovative projects they could be involved in, and the positive experiences of other employees. When a candidate feels they'll fit in well with the company and enjoy their work, they're more likely to accept the offer.

The job offer presentation process also influences the candidate's decision. Simply sending an email with the details isn't enough; a personalized presentation is recommended. A face-to-face conversation or video call allows questions to be answered immediately and conveys enthusiasm about the candidate joining the company. If possible, include a team member with whom they will work directly to reinforce the idea that their arrival will be welcomed and valued.

It's also important to consider the candidate's response time. Some companies make the mistake of pushing for an immediate decision, which can create discomfort and make the candidate feel rushed. Ideally, give them a reasonable amount of time to analyze the offer, but don't let too much time pass, as prolonged indecision may mean they're considering other options. A timeframe of two to five days is sufficient for the candidate to make an informed decision without feeling forced.

If, after presenting the offer, the candidate expresses doubts or requests modifications, it's important to be open to negotiation. In many cases, small adjustments can make the proposal much more attractive. It could be an additional bonus, a more convenient start date, or some extra benefit that doesn't represent a high cost to the company but is of great value to the candidate. The key is to understand what aspects are most important to the candidate and try to reach an agreement that benefits both parties.

If a candidate declines the offer, it's a good idea to ask them the reasons for their decision. This can help improve future proposals and better understand what talent is looking for in the market. Sometimes a candidate says no simply because they received another offer that better meets their needs, but other times, the problem may have been something the company can improve in its future hires.

Making an irresistible offer isn't just a matter of money; it's about understanding what the candidate truly values and presenting a proposal that makes them feel this is the best place to work. When a company manages to craft compelling offers, it not only increases its chances of hiring top talent but also strengthens its reputation as a place where people want to be. The key is to think beyond salary and design an offer that makes the candidate feel accepting is the best decision for their future.

Onboarding

The hiring process doesn't end when the candidate accepts the offer. In fact, one of the most critical moments begins right afterward: onboarding. This term refers to the new employee's integration into the company, a process that can make the difference between a successful onboarding and a frustrating experience for both the employee and the organization. A good onboarding process not only helps the person adapt more quickly to their new role, but also increases their commitment, motivation, and productivity from the very first days.

One of the most common mistakes in many companies is assuming that the new employee will arrive, sit at their desk, and automatically understand how everything works. Without clear guidance, they can easily feel lost, overwhelmed, or even demotivated. The key to successful onboarding is structuring it so that the person feels welcomed, understood, and supported throughout their adaptation process. To achieve this, it is essential that the company has a well-defined plan before the new employee arrives.

The first step is advance preparation. Before a new employee steps into the office or logs in for the first time in a remote environment, the company must ensure everything is ready for their arrival. This includes having their workspace set up, with their computer, login credentials, email, and any other resources they need to get started smoothly. For remote work, this means ensuring they have access to the necessary platforms and receive clear guidance on how to connect and communicate with the team.

The first day is key to onboarding. It's when employees begin to form an impression of the company, the team, and their role. To ensure this day is a positive experience, it's advisable to provide a formal welcome, either through a meeting with their direct manager or with the entire team. During this welcome, it's important to explain the company culture, its values, and what's expected of them in their new position. It's also a good opportunity to introduce them to their colleagues and help them build connections from the start.

Another crucial aspect of onboarding is clear expectations. New employees need to know what is expected of them in the first few weeks and what their primary responsibilities will be. Companies often make the mistake of assigning tasks without a detailed explanation, which can lead to confusion and anxiety. To avoid this, it's advisable to provide a work plan for the first few days or weeks, detailing their initial objectives and the steps they must take to achieve them.

Assigning a mentor or peer supporter is an effective strategy to facilitate adaptation. This person can be a more experienced colleague within the company, who is willing to guide and answer questions for the new employee during their first few weeks. Having someone they trust to turn to reduces anxiety and speeds up the integration process, as it allows the new employee to feel supported at all times.

Onboarding isn't just about the technical side of the job, but also about social integration. An employee who feels part of the team from the start is more likely to commit to the company and perform better in their role. To achieve this, it's advisable to organize informal meetings or integration activities where the new employee can get to know their colleagues better in a relaxed environment. This is especially important in companies with remote work, where distance can make connecting between employees more difficult.

The integration process should extend beyond the first week. It's advisable to conduct periodic follow-ups during the first month and up to the first three months to ensure the employee is adapting well. During these follow-ups, it's helpful to ask about their experiences, concerns, and any obstacles they encountered during their adaptation process. This not only helps resolve issues in a timely manner but also demonstrates interest in their well-being and development within the company.

Another key element of good onboarding is feedback. New employees need to know if they're moving in the right direction and if there are areas they can improve. This doesn't mean formal evaluations from the first month, but rather providing constructive feedback on their initial performance. If employees receive guidance and recognition from the start, they're more likely to feel motivated and continue working hard.

A good onboarding process not only benefits the employee, but also the company. A worker who feels welcomed and supported from day one adapts more quickly, makes fewer mistakes, and begins to contribute value to the organization in less time. On the other hand, when the integration process is poor, the employee may feel disoriented or dissatisfied, which increases the risk of resignation within the first few months. In fact, many companies lose valuable talent because they fail to invest in a good onboarding process.

Ultimately, onboarding is one of the most important phases of the hiring process and should be treated with the same seriousness and planning as candidate selection. Creating a welcoming environment, providing clear information, providing support, and providing ongoing follow-up are the keys to ensuring a new employee quickly becomes a productive and engaged member of the team. When done well, onboarding not only helps retain talent but also strengthens company culture and improves the dynamics of the entire organization.

Measuring the Success of a Hire

Hiring the right person is only the first step. To know if a hire was truly successful, it's essential to measure their impact on the company and the team. Employers often believe a hire was a good one simply because the employee performs their duties, but this is only part of the picture. A successful hire translates into productivity, engagement, adaptation to the company culture, and, in the best-case scenario, mutual growth for both the employee and the organization.

The first indicator of success is the employee's performance in their position. During the first few months, it's important to assess whether they're meeting the objectives for which they were hired and whether they're adding value to the company. This doesn't mean expecting them to be perfect from day one, but rather showing clear progress and continuous learning. To measure this, it's advisable to set concrete goals from the outset and conduct periodic reviews to see how they're progressing in adapting and completing tasks.

Another key aspect is the speed with which the new employee integrates into the team. A good employee is not only efficient in their individual work but must also be able to collaborate with their colleagues and adapt to the team dynamics. If after several weeks they still have difficulty communicating, working together, or understanding internal processes, it may be a sign that the integration isn't working as it should. To avoid this, it's important for company leaders to pay attention to how the new member interacts with others and whether they are adapting naturally.

The new employee's level of engagement is also a key indicator. An engaged employee shows enthusiasm for their job, actively participates in meetings, and contributes ideas for improving processes. If, on the other hand, after a few months, they maintain a distant attitude, avoid getting involved, or simply do the bare minimum, it's possible that hiring them wasn't the best choice. Evaluating engagement can be tricky, but a good way to do it is by observing their level of proactivity and asking their team about their perception of it.

A clear sign of a successful hiring is the employee's retention. If an employee resigns within the first few months, it's a clear sign that something went wrong with the selection process or their onboarding. High employee turnover not only represents a financial cost to the company but also affects team morale and creates instability within the organization. To reduce this risk, it's advisable to conduct follow-up interviews with the new employee to identify potential problems before they decide to leave.

The impact on team productivity is also a factor to consider. A good employee not only does their job well, but also contributes to improving the efficiency of others. If, after hiring someone, the team works better, errors are reduced, or processes are streamlined, it's a sign that the hiring was a good idea. On the other hand, if the arrival of the new member creates conflicts, slows down work, or creates tension among colleagues, it may be a sign that it wasn't the best choice.

To measure the success of a hiring process, it's also helpful to gather feedback from a variety of sources. Asking supervisors, peers, and the employee themselves about the onboarding process helps identify strengths and areas for improvement. Sometimes, an employee may be performing well but feel dissatisfied or demotivated for reasons that aren't immediately apparent. Listening to their opinions and concerns is an effective way to ensure their experience at the company is positive and productive.

Another important indicator is the impact the new hire has on the company's overall objectives. If the new hire helps achieve strategic goals, solve important problems, or improve areas that were struggling, it's a clear sign that the choice was the right one. Conversely, if after several months the company is still facing the same problems or there hasn't been any significant improvement, it's possible that the position wasn't filled with the most suitable person.

Evaluating the success of a hiring process isn't a one-time process. It requires periodic reviews and adjustments to strategies based on the results. Not every hire will be perfect, but if the company learns from each experience, it can improve its selection processes and increase the likelihood of hiring the right people in the future.

Ultimately, successful hiring isn't just measured by whether someone has accepted the offer and joined the company. It's about evaluating their performance, integration, level of commitment, and the impact they have on the organization. Only by consistently measuring these factors can we ensure that each new employee isn't just filling a vacancy, but actually contributing to the company's long-term growth and success.

Common Hiring Mistakes and How to Avoid Them

Hiring the wrong person can become a costly and frustrating problem for any company. Despite their best efforts, employers often make mistakes in the recruitment process, whether by rushing, failing to properly evaluate candidates, or neglecting key aspects of hiring. These errors can lead to high staff turnover, conflicts within the team, and even significant financial losses. To avoid these situations, it's essential to know the most common hiring mistakes and how to prevent them.

One of the most common mistakes is hiring in a hurry. Many companies try to fill a vacancy as quickly as possible and end up choosing the first person who seems like a good fit, without taking the time to evaluate several candidates. Urgency can lead to impulsive decisions, and what initially seems like a quick fix can become a long-term problem. To avoid this, it's essential to plan your hiring process in advance, clearly define the profile of the ideal candidate, and dedicate the necessary time to objectively evaluate each applicant.

Another common mistake is basing the decision solely on the resume. While experience and technical skills are important, they are not the only factors that determine whether someone is the right person for the position. Many candidates may have an impressive resume but lack the soft skills needed to fit into the company culture or work well in a team. To avoid this mistake, it's important to complement the resume review with effective interviews, practical tests, and job references that confirm whether the candidate is truly a good fit.

Blindly trusting what the candidate says in the interview is another common mistake. Some people are highly skilled at selling themselves and can give perfect answers without it meaning they're actually the best fit for the position. To avoid falling into this trap, it's advisable to ask situational questions that force the candidate to demonstrate with concrete examples how they've handled situations in previous jobs. Additionally, checking job references is a key strategy to confirm that the information provided by the candidate is truthful.

Failure to clearly define job expectations is another common problem. If the company doesn't make clear from the outset what the new employee's responsibilities, goals, and expectations are, misunderstandings and frustrations are likely to arise. This can lead to employee dissatisfaction or the company's disappointment with their performance. To avoid this, it's essential that the job offer be detailed and that the duties and expected results be clearly explained during the interview.

One mistake many companies make is ignoring organizational culture when hiring. It's not enough for a candidate to have the necessary skills; they must also fit in with the values, way of working, and team dynamics. An employee who doesn't identify with the company culture may have difficulty adapting and, in many cases, end up leaving quickly. To avoid this problem, it's important to assess whether the candidate shares the company's values and whether their personality is compatible with the work environment.

Another common mistake is neglecting the onboarding process. Companies often hire a good candidate, but then fail to provide the guidance and support necessary to integrate properly. Without a well-structured onboarding process, the new employee can feel lost, demotivated, and less productive. To avoid this, it's advisable to implement an onboarding plan that includes a proper welcome, a clear overview of their duties, and support during their first few weeks.

Not involving the right people in the hiring decision is another mistake that can lead to problems. Sometimes, the responsibility of selecting a new employee falls on a single person, increasing the risk of bias and poor decisions. To make a better selection, it's advisable to include several people in the process, such as the candidate's future supervisor and other team members with whom they will work. This allows for different perspectives and ensures that the person chosen is truly the best fit.

Offering an uncompetitive salary can also affect hiring. Many companies try to save costs by offering low salaries, which limits access to quality candidates and can lead to high staff turnover. A good employee knows their worth and won't accept a job that doesn't offer fair compensation. To avoid this problem, it's important to research market salaries and ensure the offer is attractive not only in financial terms, but also in terms of benefits and growth opportunities.

A serious mistake is not monitoring a new employee's performance. Many companies believe that the hiring process ends when the employee begins performing their duties, but this is not true. It is essential to conduct periodic evaluations to ensure the new employee is adapting well and meeting expectations. If problems are detected early, corrective measures can be taken before the situation worsens.

Finally, one of the most costly mistakes is failing to learn from bad hires. If a company realizes it has hired the wrong person, the worst thing it can do is ignore the problem and repeat the same mistakes in future selections. Every bad experience should be an opportunity to improve the hiring process. Analyzing what went wrong, identifying what signals were missed, and adjusting the selection process will allow for better decisions in the future and reduce the risk of bad hires.

Avoiding these common mistakes requires time, planning, and a strategic approach to hiring. It's not just about filling a position, but ensuring that the chosen person truly adds value to the company and becomes a productive team member. A good selection process not only saves time but also contributes to the growth and stability of the organization. Hiring wisely is not an easy task, but avoiding these mistakes can make the difference between a solid team and a business plagued by staffing issues.

www.ingramcontent.com/pod-product-compliance
Lightning Source LLC
La Vergne TN
LVHW101616210926
848480LV00009B/677